San Patricio Family Favourites

Nama's Kitchen

OEnone Elizabeth Keys

Things I've learnt from trying to cook in a family kitchen:

Don't make something for a special occasion that you have not tried before or you may be in for a nasty surprise-!

Most recipes can benefit from a little of your own innovations- it's called adding 'asterixes' in our family-!

Best to cook without too much help, as it can be a distraction & you end up burning things.

When baking it's important to know your oven.

A very useful tool is a portable kitchen timer, for when you have to do something else as well as cooking.

After very many requests, I have finally managed to put together this collection of family favourites which I dedicate to my daughters & my family.

(Alita's sketches add to the leavening in this cookery mix!)

IV

Introduction

This collection of inventions and adaptations of recipes has been compiled to remember the family food, fun and friends of Nama's San Patricio, in whose big old fashioned 'camp' kitchen, fresh cream, garlic, eggs, and classical music abounded. It is memories of cooking with pleasure and imagination, with lots of help, or no help, dealing with power cuts, strange diets and fads, but always enjoying and having the great satisfaction of a well cooked tasty meal served at a candle lit table, or one out amongst birds and flowers in a garden.

All involved had their special favourites and everyone wanted San Patricio's dulce de leche!

Happy cooking!

Contents

Introduction

Hors d'oeuvres

Eggs San Patricio

Bring to a boil:

* * 4 tbsp. peas (fresh or frozen)

Strain them into:

* * ¾ cup heavy cream
* * season with salt & pepper

Butter the mini cocottes &:

* * line the bottom with peas & cream
* * crack a fresh egg into each one

Place the cocottes in a baking tin with water. Bain-marie in the oven for about 20 min until the eggs set.

Season and serve.

Serves 4

Devilled Mushrooms

* 1 tbsp. butter
* 175 g button mushrooms cleaned & diced
* juice of ½ lemon
* 1 tbsp. flour
* 4 tbsp. top of the milk
* 1 tsp. horseradish sauce
* 2 tsp. worcestershire sauce
* 1 tsp. french dijon-style mustard
* 1 tsp. tomato purée
* salt & freshly ground pepper
* 4 slices hot buttered toast
* 1 tbsp. freshly chopped parsley

Melt the butter in a small pan. Add mushrooms & fry gently for 2 min stirring constantly.
Sprinkle in the lemon juice.
Stir in the flour & cook for 1 min then stir in the milk and the remaining ingredients. Add salt & pepper to taste.
Pile onto hot buttered toast, sprinkle with parsley & serve immediately.

Serves 4

Empanadas

Ingredients:

* 24 empanada dough discs
* ¼ kg finely minced meat

Place the meat in a large frying pan.

Filling:

Add chopped small:
* ½ onion
* 5 garlic cloves
* 1 tbsp. parsley
* ¼ red bell pepper
* ¼ green bell pepper
* 1 hardboiled egg
* 10 olives
* 1 tbsp. whole raisins

When it begins to stick to the pan, add:
* a ladle spoon of stock, mix well
* season with salt & pepper

Lay pastry discs out on a board.
Fill each disc with 1 large tbsp. of prepared
mince meat. Fold & seal.
Fry in hot oil or bake in oven.
When cooked sprinkle with salt & serve at once.

Makes 24 small emapanadas

Little Chive Pies

Pastry:

* 2½ cups plain flour
* a pinch of salt
* 175 g butter
* 75 g lard
* milk, for glazing

Filling:

* 1 cup full fat cream cheese or curd cheese
* 2 to 3 tsp. chopped fresh chives or
* 2 tsp. dried chives
* salt & black pepper

Sift the flour & salt into a mixing bowl. Cut in the fat & rub in the mixture with your fingertips until it resembles breadcrumbs. With a knife, mix in a little cold water (about 4 to 5 tbsp) until the mixture just sticks together.

Gather into a ball, wrap in foil & chill in the fridge for at least an hour.

To make the pies:

Roll our the pastry to about 3mm|0.1 in. thickness.
Use a round fluted cutter & cut into 18 rounds, &
then with a 5.5 cm|2.2 in. round cutter cut another
18 rounds, re-rolling the pastry as necessary.

Put the filling ingredients in a bowl & mix thoroughly. Line some patty tins with the large rounds of
pastry. Smooth some filling into each round. Moist-
en the underside of the smaller rounds & put on top,
pressing down lightly at the edges.

Heat the oven to 425 F|220 C. Make a small slit on
the top of each pie. Brush with milk & bake in the
centre of the oven for about 2 min. Leave to cool
in the tins for 5-10 min & then gently- as the pastry is deliciously crumbly - ease them out with a
round-bladed knife.

Makes 18

Grapefruit & Capsicum Cocktail

* 2 grapefruits
* 150 g cheddar cheese
* ½ small red or green bell pepper
* juice of grapefruit
* 1 tbsp. olive oil
* sugar (optional)
* seasoning
* garnish with lettuce

Halve the grapefruit.
Remove the segments carefully, put them in bowl &
discard any pips, cut away the skin.
Dice the cheddar cheese & chop the red pepper,
discarding the core & seeds, mix with the grapefruit.
Pour the juice from the grapefruit into a separate
bowl & blend with olive oil, sugar & seasoning.

Pour the dressing over the cheese mixture & leave
for about 30 min for the dressing to flavour the
other ingredients.

Line the halved grapefruit cases with lettuce
Pile the salad in the centre.
Serve with crisp toast or brown bread & butter.

Variations:
- Use orange segments & serve in sundae glasses.
- Top halved peaches with grated cheese or fill centre of pineapple rings with cheese blended with mayonnaise.

Serve ½ a fruit per person

Chutney Toasts

- Good homemade chutney or fruit preserve
- Any type of cracker or dainty crisp toasts

Spread a good dollop of softened cream cheese on cracker or toast.
Cover this with a spoonful of chutney or preserve.

Serve a toast per person

Pears and Prosciutto

* 6 pears
* prosciutto (thinly sliced)
* peel pear, leave stem, cut in 4

Pear must remain standing.
* dribble lemon juice over all of it
(this maintains the color & flavour of the pear)
* wrap prosciutto around it

Place on plate & serve.

Serves 6

Avocado

A good hot weather hors d'oeuvre.
The delicate flavour of avocado calls for a light
dressing.

Slice your avocado in half.
Brush the fruit with lemon juice.

In the centre, where the pit of the avocado sat,

Fill with french dressing:

* olive oil
* lemon juice
* salt & black pepper

Have more dressing in a little pitcher on hand.

Serve ½ or whole avocado per person.

Courgette Timbales

* sunflower oil for greasing
* 700 g courgettes (zucchini)
* 3 eggs, beaten
* 1 tbsp. chopped fresh basil
* ½ cup ricotta cheese
* salt & freshly ground black pepper

Tomato Salsa:

* 350 g tomatoes, peeled & sliced
* 1 red onion, finely chopped
* 1 tbsp. chopped fresh basil
* 1 tbsp. olive oil
* 1 tsp. lime juice

Mix together tomatoes, onion, basil, olive oil, lime juice, salt & pepper. Chill until required.

Oil six ½ cup ramekins.

Trim ends from courgettes. Cut remaining courgettes into slices. Steam slices over a saucepan of boiling water for 2 min until soft. Spread on kitchen paper & pat dry. Steam sliced courgettes for 3 - 5 min until soft.

Preheat oven to 200°C | 400°F.

Press out as much moisture as possible from courgette slices & place in a blender with the eggs, basil & ricotta. Season with salt & pepper. Process to a coarse purée.

Line ramekins with courgette strips. Fill with purée, fold over ends of courgette strips & cover with foil. Place ramekins in a roasting tin & pour in 1 cm | 0.4 in. boiling water. Bake for 10 - 15 min until set. Leave for 5 min turn out & serve with tomato salsa.

Serves 6

Hearts of Palm in Creamy Sauce

* 1 tin heart of palm (cut into chunks)

Make a sauce with:

* 4 tbsp. lemon based mayonnaise
* 1 tbsp. ketchup

(Basic Proportion)

Mix well, add:

* freshly ground black pepper

Pour over hearts of palm.
Calculate about 2 large tbsp. per person.
Serve on a crisp lettuce leaf & sprinkle with
ciboulette (cut with scissors).

Serves 4 - 6

Soups

Cream of Celery Soup

Cook together until vegetables are soft:

* 1 cup chopped celery, stalks & leaves
* 1 slice of onion (or more)
* 2 cups chicken broth or water

Rub through a sieve, without draining or
whirl in an electric blender.

Add:

* 1 ½ cups top of milk or cream
* salt & pepper to taste

Heat slowly. Blend if you prefer a thicker, smoother
soup.
Serve with grated gruyère cheese.

Serves 4 - 6

Note   Keep clean vegetable skins & stalks & bits, to
add when making a broth, it adds flavour.

Beetroot Soup

* 1 onion, coarsely grated
* 1 large carrot, coarsely grated
* 454 g raw beets, peeled, coarsely grated
* fresh parsley sprig
* 1 bay leaf
* 4 cups chicken stock
* 1 egg white
* juice ½ lemon
* salt & pepper to taste
* thin lemon slices to garnish

In a large saucepan, combine all ingredients except egg white & lemon.
Bring to a boil, cover & simmer 30 min.
Strain soup in a colander set over a bowl. Clean pan & return liquid to pan. To clear soup, bring to a boil.
Whisk egg white in a small bowl, then stir into soup. Simmer gently 15 min.
Strain soup through a muslin-lined sieve set over a bowl. Stir in lemon juice. Cool & refrigerate until chilled. Season soup with salt & pepper.
Garnish with lemon slices.

Serves 4 - 6

Cold Watercress & Almond Soup

* 2 large bunches watercress
* 2 tbsp. butter
* 1 small onion
* 2 cups vegetable stock
* ⅓ cup blanched almonds, toasted, ground
* 1 tbsp. + 1 tsp. cornstarch
* 2 cups milk
* salt & pepper to taste
* flaked almonds, lightly toasted, to garnish

Wash watercress. Reserve a few sprigs to garnish.
Cut away any coarse stalks & chop the remainder.
Melt butter in a large saucepan. Sautée onion in
butter until soft. Add watercress. Cook 2 min then
stir in chicken stock. Cover & simmer for another
10 minutes.
Blend watercress mixture to a purée. Clean pan &
return purée to pan. Stir in ground almonds. In
small bowl, blend cornstarch with a little milk. Add
to watercress mixture, then stir in remaining milk.
Simmer gently over low heat, stirring constantly for
5 min or until smooth. Remove from heat & cool.
Refrigerate at least 4 hours or overnight.
Garnish soup with flaked almonds and reserved
watercress sprigs.

Œnone's French Onion Soup

* 2 tbsp. butter
* 2 tbsp. olive oil
* 6 large onions, thinly sliced
* 3 cloves of garlic, crushed
* pinch of sugar
* 5 cups beef stock
* 1 cup red wine
* 1 bay leaf
* salt & pepper to taste
* 6 thick slices french bread
* 1 tsp. dijon-style mustard
* ¾ cup shredded gruyère cheese
* 2 large tbsp. brandy

Heat butter & oil in a large saucepan.
Add onions, garlic & sugar. Cook over medium heat about 20 min stirring occasionally, until onions are a deep golden brown.

Add stock & bay leaf, 1 cup of red wine & slowly bring to a boil. Simmer 25 min. Remove bay leaf and season with salt & pepper.

Toast bread on each side & spread with mustard. Ladle soup into 4 heat-proof bowls, add brandy & top with toast. Pile cheese onto toast & toast under grill until cheese is melted & bubbling. Serve at once.

Serves 6

Garden Club's Cream of Carrot Soup

Cook:

*   5 thinly sliced carrots

In:

* 2 tbsp. butter
* 1 tbsp. sugar
* salt
* ½ cup water

As they are cooking, make a white sauce with:

* 2 tbsp. butter
* 2 tbsp. flour
* salt, pepper, nutmeg
* 2 ½ cups milk

Bring to the boil.
Once the carrots are cooked, blend them into the
white sauce. Reserve some carrot rounds for decoration.

Add:

* ¼ litre heavy cream
* Season with salt & pepper

Heat and serve.

Serves 6

Cream of Cucumber Soup

Peel slice & seed:
- 3 large cucumbers

Cook 10 min in:
- 2 tbsp. butter

Stir in:
- 3 tbsp. flour

Add gradually:
- 3 cups chicken stock

Scald:
- 1 cup milk
- 1 slice onion
- few grains mace or nutmeg

Combine the mixtures. Rub through a sieve or whirl in an electric blender.

Reheat to the boiling point. Stir in:
- ½ cup cream
- 2 egg yolks, slightly beaten
- season to taste with salt & pepper

For chilled cucumber soup omit the egg yolks. chill before adding the cream.
Season with a few drops of angostura bitters.

Serves 4 - 6

Sharp Pesto Soup

* ¼ cup + 3 tbsp. olive oil
* 1 small onion, finely chopped
* 340 g zucchini, diced
* ½ cup risotto rice
* 5 cups hot chicken stock
* salt & pepper to taste
* 30 g fresh basil leaves
* ¼ cup pine nuts
* 2 garlic cloves
* ¼ tsp. salt
* ½ cup freshly grated parmesan cheese

Parmesan Croutons:

* 2 tbsp. butter
* 2 slices bread
* ¼ cup of the grated parmesan cheese

Butter the bread & spread with ¼ cup parmesan cheese, cut in cubes & toast in hot oven.

Heat 2 tbsp. of oil in a large saucepan:

Gently cook onion & zucchini 3 - 4 min or until softened. Stir in rice & coat grains with oil. Pour in hot stock & bring to a boil. Simmer 10 min or until rice is tender. Season with salt & pepper.

Meanwhile, to prepare Pesto Sauce:

Process remaining olive oil, basil leaves, pine nuts, garlic & ¼ tsp. salt to a purée in a blender.

Transfer mixture to a small bowl & beat in ¼ cup of the cheese. Add 1 tsp. pesto to each serving of soup.

Serves 4 - 6

Zucchini & Tomato Soup

* 2 tbsp | 30 g butter
* 1 medium-size onion, finely chopped
* 340 g zucchini, coarsely grated
* 1 garlic clove, crushed
* 2½ cups vegetable stock
* 1 can | 400 g chopped & peeled tomatoes
* 2 tbsp. chopped fresh mixed herbs (optional)
* salt & pepper to taste
* ¼ cup whipping cream
* fresh basil leaves to garnish

Melt butter in a large saucepan. Cook onion in butter until soft.
Stir in zucchini & garlic & cook 4 - 5 min.
Stir in stock & tomatoes with their juice.
Bring to a boil & simmer 15 min.

Add a spoonful of whipped cream to each serving.

Serves 4 - 6

Gazpacho

Make the day before you serve.

Grind a clove (or more) of garlic with:

* ½ tsp. of salt

Add:

* 2 tbsp. of oil
* 5 ripe tomatoes chopped in cubes
* 1 large onion chopped
* ¼ tsp. pepper
* ¼ tsp. paprika
* 1½ tbsp. vinegar

Blend.
Let sit for an hour or more, then sieve, add more salt if necessary.

Add:

* ¼ cup dry bread crumbs.

Serve in cups, adding:

* an ice cube to each one.

Accompany with croutons, chopped cucumber & chopped green bell pepper.

Serves 6

Grilled Pepper & Aubergine Soup

* 2 large red peppers
* 1 large aubergine
* 6 tbsp. olive oil
* 1 large onion
* 2 garlic cloves
* 1 tsp. grated lemon rind
* 1 tbsp. chopped fresh thyme
* 1 tsp. dried oregano
* 400 g can chopped tomatoes
* 3 cups vegetable or chicken stock
* 1 bay leaf
* 2 tbsp. chopped fresh basil
* salt & pepper

For the saffron cream:

* small pinch of saffron strands
* 1 egg yolk
* 1 garlic clove, crushed
* ½ tsp. cayenne pepper
* 2 tsp. lemon juice
* ¾ cup olive oil

Preheat the grill. Quarter, core & deseed the red peppers. Brush with a little olive oil & grill on each side until charred & tender. Transfer to a plate, cover with a cloth & leave until cool enough to handle. Peel the peppers & roughly chop the flesh.

Thinly slice the aubergine lengthways. Brush with oil & grill on each side until charred & tender. Leave until cool enough to handle, then chop roughly.

Peel & chop the onion & garlic. Heat the remaining oil in a large pan, add the onion, garlic, lemon rind, thyme, oregano & fry, stirring for 10 min until browned. Add the peppers, aubergine, tomatoes, stock & bay leaf. Bring to the boil, cover & simmer for 20 min. Discard the bay leaf.

Meanwhile, make the saffron cream. Put the saffron in a small bowl, pour on 1 tbsp. boiling water & leave to soak for 5 min in a bowl. Whisk the egg yolk with the garlic, cayenne, lemon juice & seasoning until pale & slightly thickened. Gradually whisk in the oil, beating until thick. Stir in the saffron liquid & season to taste.

Transfer the soup to a blender or food processor.
Add the basil & work until smooth. Return to the
pan & heat through. Adjust the seasoning & pour
into warmed soup bowls. Spoon a little saffron
cream onto each portion, garnish with basil leaves &
serve at once.

Variation:

Replace the aubergine with 2 yellow peppers & grill
as above. Divide all other ingredients in half & cook
in separate pans, adding the red peppers to one &
the yellow peppers to the other. Cook until tender
& purée separately to give 2 different coloured pepper soups. Serve half of each in each bowl, swirling
them attractively, & garnish with saffron cream.
Cooking time 45 - 50 min.

Serves 4 - 6

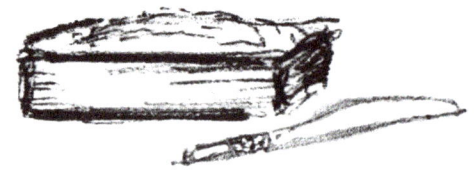

Main Courses

Veal Olives

* 6 thin beef cutlets
* 3 tbsp. butter
* 2 large onions
* 1 small bouquet garni
* 3 tomatoes
* ½ cup dry white wine
* ¾ cup stock
* 2 to 4 button onions
* 1 tbsp. butter
* 2 tsp. sugar
* 1 tbsp. potato flour or
* 2 tbsp. cornstarch
* ½ cup madeira

Stuffing:

* 455 g sausage meat
* 140 g ground veal
* 1 cup dry bread crumbs, moistened in milk
* 2 shallots
* 2 scallions
* dash of dried thyme
* 3 tbsp. chopped parsley
* salt & pepper
* 1 egg
* garnish with chopped parsley

Stuffing:

Mix the sausage meat with the minced veal, bread-crumbs, the chopped shallots & spring onions, thyme, parsley & seasoning. Bind this stuffing with the beaten egg.

Flatten the escalopes with a rolling pin or meat mallet. Place the stuffing in the centre of each & roll up into a parcel so that the stuffing is firmly enclosed. Tie with string or secure with toothpicks.

Heat a knob of butter in a casserole. Sautée the veal olives with the chopped large onions, let them brown well on all sides. Add the bouquet garni & the tomatoes, peeled, deseeded & crushed. Leave to cook for 10 min then moisten with the wine & stock. Season, cover & cook in a moderate oven of 180 C|350 F or on stove top for approx. 45 mins.

To glaze the onions:

Remove the outer skin of the button onions, & cook with 4 tbsp. water, the tbsp. of butter & the sugar. Leave until the juice caramelises. Then coat the onions with the glaze.

Tranfer the veal olives to a heated serving dish & surround with the glazed onions.

Strain the sauce from the veal through a sieve & thicken over a gentle heat, stirring in the potato flour or cornflour mixed with the madeira. Bring to the boil, stirring continuously, & pour over the veal olives. Sprinkle with chopped parsley to serve.

Serves 4 - 6.

Bife Irlandés

Cut into thin cutlets:

* 1 Kg of beefsteak

In a heavy saucepan put:

* 2 tbsp. oil
* 2 tbsp. butter

When it's hot add:

* 2 tbsp. caster sugar, stirring gently.

When it turns caramel color, stir in:

* 2 tbsp. flour

Salt & pepepr the steaks & add one at a time. Pour a ladle full of stock over every 4 steaks.
Cook gently over a low flame, with the lid on.

When they are tender add:

* 4 tbsp. of chopped olives.

And cook for a further 10 min.

Serve with mashed potatoes.

Serves 6

Perdiz en Escabeche

Clean, wash & season with salt & pepper:

* 7 perdices

Place them in pot, add:

* 8 carrots cut in julienne slices
* 1 tsp. black peppercorns
* 3 bay leaves
* 8 garlic cloves
* 1 cup vinegar
* 1 glass of wine
* 3 cups oil
* season with coarse salt

Cover the pot & leave to simmer slowly until well cooked.

10 min before taking them off stove, add:

* 4 lemon slices
* ½ a sliced onion

Serve hot or cold.
The simpler the seasoning of these perdices, the more delicate the flavour.

Serves 7

Tucco de Paloma San Patricio

* 30 to 40 dove breasts

Braise them on either side on a hot skillet. Between batches pour a little stock & scrape what is stuck to the pan & set that juice aside.

Meanwhile, slice 6 large onions & sautée in:

* 2 tbsp. oil
* 2 tbsp. butter

Add:

* 1 whole head of garlic (with tips cut off)

When onion is transparent & begining to brown,
Add:

* 2 cups of peeled diced tomatoes
* ½ tsp. sugar

Add herbs:

Bouquet garni (rosemary, basil & most importantly oregano) or any other herb of your choice, cover & let bubble gently.

Meanwhile cut the dove breasts into little cubes, to be added to the tomato & onion sauce when it's nearly ready (about ½ hour before serving). Overcooking the dove makes it tough.

Before serving squeeze the pulp out of the garlic and mix in well.

Serve over any good pasta & sprinkle with coarsely grated parmesan or any other strong flavoured cheese.

Serves 6

Note:

Tomato sauces are good cooked with a tsp. of sugar.

Steak & Kidney Pie

Cut in fair sized cubes:

* 1 Kg beef

And braise in unbuttered pan.

Meanwhile fry:

* 6 sliced onions in
* 2 tbsp. butter
* dash of oil

Let the onions brown & sprinkle with:

* 3 tbsp. flour

Stir & mix well. Put this in the pan with the meat & add 2 ladles full of good meat stock. Put some stock in the frying pan & and pour this onto the meat as well.

Sautee in butter & set aside:

* 300 g sliced mushrooms

Chop:

* ½ kidney very small

Braise with about:

* 2 tbsp. lemon juice

When browned add:

* 1 tbsp. flour & mix well

Add to the meat:

* a head of garlic, peeled with tips cut off (don't separate the cloves).

Cover & simmer gently, adding more stock as the liquid gets absorbed. Half way through the cooking add 1½ to 2 cups of a good red wine.

When cooked, add mushrooms, a dash of Lee & Perrins & salt & pepper to taste. Squeeze out the soft flesh of the garlic & mix in well.

Place in ovenproof dish with a coffee cup upside down, in the centre, to help support the following crust, made with:

Pie crust:

* 8 tbsp. piled of flour
* 2 tsp. piled baking powder
* ½ tsp. salt
* 4 tbsp. piled butter, lard or pigs fat

Mix dry ingredients, add fat & mix with a fork or fingers. Don't work too much.

Add enough water to make a paste this should come cleanly off the bowl.

Roll out to size of your baking dish, with a margin and place on your pie dish.

Wet the fork to decorate around the edge & brush the top with egg yolk or water.

Cook about 15 to 30 min in a hot oven.

Serves 6

Note:

Use cream that is beginning to turn instead of butter for pastry & scones or to add to stews.

Hungarian Paprika Chicken

* 1 chicken
* 1 onion
* little grated lemon rind
* 4 cups water
* 4 to 5 peppercorns
* little salt
* bouquet garni

Sauce:

* 30 g butter
* 1 cup button mushrooms
* ¼ cup flour
* 1 to 2 tbsp. paprika
* 2⅔ cup stock
* ⅔ cup thick cream
* seasoning

Joint the chicken.
Chop the onion.

Put the lemon rind, chicken, water & onion into a pan with the pepper-corns, salt & bouquet garni. Simmer until the chicken is tender. This takes about 45 min.
Lift the chicken from the stock, strain the stock & keep 2⅔ cups for the sauce. Either dice the chicken or keep in 4 joints.
Heat the butter in the pan. Toss the mushrooms in the hot butter for a few minutes. Lift onto a plate.

Add:

Flour & paprika, stir well for 2 - 3 min over a low heat, then gradually blend in the stock, bring to the boil & cook, stirring until thickened. Put the chicken & mushrooms into the sauce. Simmer until thoroughly heated. Add some of the cream & seasoning and simmer for 4-5 min, do not boil. Top with the remainder of the cream.

Serves 4 - 6

Sweet & Sour Tongue

* clean a fair sized tongue

Boil for about 2½ to 3 hours until tender with:

* bouquet garni
* 3 carrots
* 1 onion
* salt

Pierce with fork & when tender, it is done
(tongue needs to be well cooked).
Let cool slightly & peel.
Cut in thin slices.
Place on flat pyrex & drizzle with Raisin Sauce (it
can be re-heated when ready to serve).

Raisin Sauce, mix:

* ½ cup brown sugar
* ½ tbsp. mustard (Coleman's)
* ½ tbsp. flour

Add:

* ¼ cup seedless raisins
* ¼ cup vinegar
* 1¾ cup water

Cook slowly to a syrup, makes about 1½ cups.
Best served in conjunction with boiled potatoes with
mustard sauce.

Serves 6

Roasted Beef Sirloin

* 1 Kg sirloin with fat removed.

Put on baking tin & baste all over with oil.
Season with salt & pepper.
The less you season it, the better the delicate flavour of the meat.
Put in a hot oven for 20 min for a medium to rare roast.
Turn it once whilst cooking, to braise evenly. When cooked remove from baking tin & keep warm whilst making the gravy.

For the Gravy:

* Put the baking tin on 2 stove tops

Add:

* 2 ladles of stock
* 2 tbsp. of flour (previously liquified with milk or stock)

Bring to a boil & season with salt & pepper.
Adjust flavour with either more stock, or cream.
Serve meat immediately accompanied by roasted potatoes, yorkshire pudding & the gravy.
This meal should be served the minute it is ready.
It does not improve with re-heating, though the meat is very good cold.

Serves 4 - 6

Chicken Basque

* 1.75 Kg chicken, jointed into 8 pieces
* 2 large red peppers
* 1 very large or 2 medium onions
* 50 g sun-dried tomatoes in oil
* 2 to 3 tbsp. extra virgin olive oil
* 2 large garlic cloves, chopped
* 150 g chorizo sausage, skinned & cut into 1 cm slices
* 1 cup brown basmati rice
* 1 cup & 1 tbsp. chicken stock (made from the giblets)
* ⅔ cup dry white wine
* 1 level tbsp. tomato purée
* ½ tsp. hot paprika
* 50 g pitted black olives, halved
* ½ large orange, peeled & cut into wedges
* salt & freshly milled black pepper

Season chicken joints with salt & pepper. Add oil to the casserole, when hot add onion & peppers & brown a little (about 5 min). Next brown the chicken joints & then remove them.

Add the garlic, chorizo & dried tomatoes and stir
until the garlic is pale golden & the chorizo has
taken on some color.
Next stir in the rice, and when the grains have a
good coating of oil, remove.
Add the stock, wine, tomato purée & paprika.

As soon as everything has reached simmering point,
turn the heat down to a gentle simmer. Add a little
more seasoning, then place the chicken gently on
top of everything, sprinkle the herbs over all & scatter the olives & wedges of orange in among them.

Cover with a tight-fitting lid and cook over gentle
heat until chicken is nearly done.

10 min before serving:
   * add rice, cook & serve.

Serves 4

Perdiz en Champagne

* 6 perdices, salt, pepper
* 100 g butter
* 100 g diced onion
* 150 g champignons (sautéed in butter)
* ½ bottle demi-sec champagne
* ½ litre white sauce (seasoned with 1 meat cube bouillon, nutmeg, salt & pepper)
* ½ litre heavy cream

Clean the perdices and braise them evenly on a hot skillet.

In another pan, fry the onion & the butter. Add the perdices (seasoned with salt & pepper) into this pan & move around for 10 min. Pour the champagne over them & cook a while.

Mix the white sauce with the heavy cream & add to the perdiz pot. Cover the pan, finish cooking & before serving add the champignons.

Cooking time about 1½ hours.

Serves 6

Desserts

Poire Cardinale

Peel, but leave the stems of:

* 6 whole pears
Cook in ½ litre red wine.

When the pears are tender, add:

* 12 tbsp. sugar
Cook a little longer.

Remove pears.
Thicken the wine syrup by cooking a little longer
Add more wine to taste
Place pears in a dish & cover with the syrup,
the syrup must not be too thin.
Serve with fresh cream.

Serves 6

Note   Always when cooking fruit do not add sugar
until fruit is tender.

Pineapple Varleise

Drain & cut in chunks:

* 450 g tin of pineapples

Cover with icing sugar & add:

* 2 tbsp. rum
* 2 tbsp. cointreau

Put in fridge for one hour.

Before serving, whip up:

* ¼ litre fresh cream
* 2 tbsp. icing sugar
* 1 tbsp. kirsch

Fold in the pineapple mix & return to fridge.

Serves 4 - 6

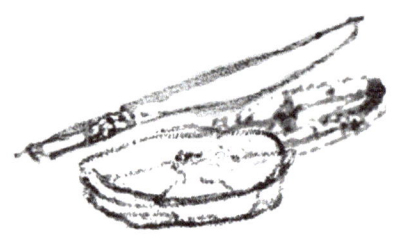

Flan Keys

* 1 tin condensed milk or
  1 cup dulce de leche
* the same cup or tin measure of milk
* 3 eggs
* ½ cup sugar

Beat the eggs thoroughly. Add:

* condensed milk or dulce de leche &
* milk

Mix well.

Melt in a pan:

* ½ cup sugar

Until caramel color

Add:

* ¼ cup of hot water

boil until a fine thread drips from spoon

Stir well until sugar is disolved & then cook until caramel coloured.

Pour into your bowl & let set.

Fill with the milk & egg mixture & place in oven in bain-marie.

Cook very slowly for 1½ hours. Let cool before turning out onto serving dish.

Serve with dulce de leche.

Serves 4 - 5

Rice Pudding

Cook slowly uncovered until creamy:

* 1 litre full fat milk
* ¼ cup rice
* $\frac{1}{3}$ cup sugar

Stir until the sugar melts & cook slowly, stirring occasionally to make sure the milk is not sticking.

In about an hour it should be ready and the rice should be tender & the milk will have started to thicken.

Serve hot or cold (best tepid) with grated lemon rind or cinnamon sprinkled on top or accompanied with dulce de leche, strawberry or peach jam.

Serves 4-5

Crème Brûlée

* 2 cups fresh double cream
* 4 egg yolks
* ½ cup sugar
* 1 tsp. vanilla essence

Put the cream in bain-marie & bring to just below boiling point.

Meanwhile put:

The egg yolks, ¼ cup of the caster sugar & the vanilla essence in a mixing bowl & beat thorougly.
Pour in the cream & stir to combine.
Pour the mixture into a shallow baking dish & place in a roasting tin half full of hot water.
Bake in a cool oven 150 C|300 F for 1 hour or until set. When set, remove from the Bain-marie & let cool.
Chill in the refrigerator for several hours, preferably overnight.
Sprinkle the top of the crème brûlée with the remaining sugar & put under a preheated hot grill until the sugar turns to caramel.
Leave to cool before serving.
This can also be made in individual little bowls.

Serves 4

Creamy Apple Tart

You can vary with pears or apricots when in season.

Pastry:

* 1¼ cup plain four
* 3 tbsp. icing sugar
* 100 g butter, plus extra for greasing
* 1 tbsp. water

Filling:

* 675 g Cox's or green cooking apples
* juice of ½ lemon
* 3 tbsp. caster sugar
* 25 g butter
* finely grated rind & juice of 1 orange
* ¾ cup double cream
* 2 tbsp. demerara sugar

To make the pastry, sift the flour & icing sugar into a bowl. Gently melt the butter with the water in a saucepan & pour on the flour & icing sugar, mixing with a wooden spoon to make a soft dough. Butter a 23 cm | 9 in. fluted, loose-based flan tin. Take the warm dough & put it in the flan tin. press it out with your fingers & line the tin evenly, passing a rolling pin over the rim to neaten the edge. Chill in the fridge for at least 30 min.

Heat the oven to 400 F | 200 C. Bake the pastry blind in the centre of the oven for 25 - 30 min until the pastry is browned in the centre as well as on the sides.

While the pastry is cooking start to prepare the filling: Peel the apples & cut them into medium-size slices. Put them in a bowl & mix with the lemon juice & caster sugar. Melt the butter in a large frying pan. Add the apple mixture & cook over medium heat, stirring gently, for about 8-12 min until the apples are tender, but not mushy. Using a slotted spoon, take up the apples & put them in the baked pastry case. Put the grated orange rind & juice in the pan with the remaining apple juice. Bubble for 30 sec, remove from the heat, add the cream & stir. Return to the heat & bubble briskly for 1 min. Spoon this slightly thickened cream over the apples.

Sprinkle the tart with the demerara sugar, push the tart out of the flan tin &, still on its flan tin base, put on to a serving plate. Serve either lukewarm, which is nicest, or cool (but don't chill).

Serves 6 - 7

Banana Almond Fool

* ½ lemon
* ½ orange
* 2 ripe bananas
* 15 g ground almonds
* 15 g blanched almonds
* 1 cup thick cream
* 1 overflowing tbsp. caster sugar

Decoration:

* 15 g blanched almonds
* 1 tbsp. demerara sugar

Grate the rind very finely from the lemon & orange,
only taking the top 'zest'.
Squeeze out the lemon & orange juice.
Mash 1 banana, adding most of the fruit juice.
Blend with the ground almonds

Chop the blanched almonds. Whip the cream until
it just holds its shape.
Blend with the banana mixture & caster sugar
Put into individual heat-resistant serving dishes &
chill well.

Slice the remaining banana, dip in the remaining
fruit juice, spoon over the fool.
Halve the almonds, sprinkle over the bananas & add
the brown sugar.
Brown under the grill then chill again. serve as cold
as possible.

To blanch almonds:
Put into boiling water for 1-2 min, remove, cool, then
take off the skins.

Serves 4

Brandy Ice Cream

Topped with crunchy caramelised almonds.

Ice cream:
* whites of 2 large eggs
* ¾ cup + 1 tbsp. demerara sugar
* ⅓ cup water
* 1 tsp. vanilla essence
* 3 to 5 tbsp. brandy
* 1¾ cups whipping cream
* a good pinch of salt

Caramelized almond top:
* 2 tbsp. caster sugar
* 50 g flaked almonds

Whisk the egg whites in a large bowl with the salt until they begin to stand in soft peaks. Dissolve the demerara sugar with the water in a saucepan, stirring over a low heat, then increase the heat & boil fiercely without stirring for 3 min. Pour immediately onto the egg whites in a thin stream, whisking all the time with an electric whisk at high speed, until the mixture is fairly thick & looks like a very smooth meringue mixture.

In separate bowl, whisk the cream until thick, but not too stiff, and then gently but thoroughly fold it into the egg white mixture with a metal spoon. Pour the mixture in a 1.6 litre freezer proof serving bowl & freeze for at least 5 hours, or several days if you want, before eating.

For the almond top:
Mix the caster sugar with the flaked almonds in a little bowl. Heat an ungreased frying pan until quite hot, then tip in the sugar & almonds & stir around constantly for only a min or so until the almonds are golden brown & caramelised. Spoon them out onto a wooden board & dig about as they cool to separate them as much as possible.

Before serving the ice cream, sprinkle the almonds all over the top.

Serves 8 - 10

Alita's Chocolate Mousse

* 250 g plain chocolate
* 3 tbsp. strong black coffee
* 6 eggs
* ¾ cup caster sugar
* 1 tbsp. rum

Break the chocoloate into small pieces, place in a
pan with the coffee & melt over a pan of hot water.
until creamy.
Break the eggs, separating the yolks from the whites.
Beat the yolks with half the sugar until pale &
creamy.
Add the rum & combine with the melted chocolate.
Whisk the egg whites until they form stiff peaks,
sprinkling them gradually with the rest of the sugar.
Fold carefully into the chocolate cream mixture.

Chill in the refrigerator until ready to serve.

Serves 6

Margaret's Steam Pudding

* weigh 3 eggs

Use the same weight of:

* sugar
* flour
* butter
* 1 tsp. vanilla essence
* 1 tsp. baking powder

Cream the butter with the sugar.
Add the eggs one at a time & the vanilla.
Beat in the flour & baking powder & a dash of milk.
Line a funnel cake pan with marmalade
& pour the mixture in.
Cook in bain-marie for 1½ hours in a hot oven.
Turn out, upside down & serve hot.

Serves 4

Teas

Shortbread

* 1½ cups flour
* 150 g butter
* ¼ cup sugar

Place all ingredients in a bowl and work together
until quite smooth.

Roll out until about ½ cm | ¼ in. thick.

Cut into squares or rounds.

Prick tops gently with a fork.

Put onto a buttered baking dish & cook in a moder-
ate oven of 350 F | 175 C for about 20 - 25 min until
golden but not toasted.

Remove from the oven & whilst hot, sprinkle
with sugar.

Makes about 25

Caramel Cake

Caramelize over low heat, stirring constantly:
* ¾ cup sugar

Dissolve with:
* ½ cup water

Add:
* 1 cup milk
* 1 tsp. vanilla

Beat until creamy:
* 75 g butter

Add gradually:
* 1 cup sugar

Add:
* 2 eggs well beaten

Sieve:
* 3¼ cups modified flour
* 3 tsp. baking powder
* ½ tsp. salt

And add alternating with the milk and the syrup.

Pour into 2 round 22x3 cm | 9x1 in. pans and place in a 350 F | 175 C oven & bake for about 30 min.

Notes
1. If modified flour is not comercially available.
Sieve 3 times:
* 5 parts flour with 1 part cornflour.
2. As a general rule bake cakes in a hot oven for the first 20 mins & then turn heat down to moderate.

Sultana Cake

* 225 g sultanas
* 100 g butter cut in small pieces
* ¾ cup + 1 tbsp. sugar
* 2 small beaten eggs
* a little almond essence
* 1¾ cup self-raising flour (or 2½ tsp. of baking powder with non-raising flour)
* pinch of salt
* 50 g chopped nuts (optional)

Note   If using nuts, reduce quantity of sultanas to 175 g.

Cover sultanas with water & soak overnight. Next day, bring to the boil. Strain sultanas & mix them, while hot, into butter.
Add sugar, eggs & almond essence. Sift in flour & salt. Lastly, add chopped nuts, if desired. Mix well.
Grease a 20 cm | 8 in. round tin & line bottom with greased, greaseproof paper. Tip cake mixture in & smooth the top.
Bake in a moderate oven, 350 F | 180 C for 30 min. Lower heat to slow, 300 F | 150 C, until firm to touch in centre.
(Is nice with a thin glaze of jam spread over it, decorated with walnuts).

Smash

For the shortbread:
* 150 g butter
* 1 cup + 1 tbsp. sugar
* 2 cups + 2 tbsp. flour

For topping:
* 100 g plain chocolate broken into pieces

For the filling:
* 100 butter
* 1 cup + 1 tbsp. sugar
* 2 tbsp. golden syrup
* 1 large can condensed milk (or equivalent size pot of dulce de leche)

Shortbread:

Cream the butter & sugar together in a mixing bowl. Work in the flour with a wooden spoon. Press into a greased 30x20 cm | 12x8 in. swiss roll tin & bake in a moderate oven 180 C | 350 F for 15 - 20 min or until the shortbread is golden in color. Remove from the oven & leave to cool.

Filling:

Put all the ingredients in a saucepan & heat gently until the sugar has dissolved, stirring occasionally. Increase the heat & boil the mixture for 5 min, stirring continuously. Remove from the heat, leave to cool for 1 min, then pour onto the cooled shortbread base. Leave to set.

Melt the chocolate in a small heatproof bowl over a pan of hot water. Spread over the set filling. Mark into serving portions, fingers or squares, & leave until quite cold & set before removing from the tin.

Makes 25

Scones

* 2 cups flour
* 2 tbsp. heavy sour cream
* ½ to 1 tsp. salt (to taste)
* 1 tbsp. sugar
* 4 tsp. baking powder
* ½ to 1 cup milk or thin sour cream

Sieve:

Flour, baking powder & salt. Rub in the heavy cream & work with hands until it disappears, handling as little as possible.

Work dough for scones very lightly.

Add the milk rapidly & roll out to an inch thick on a marble slab. The pastry should be wettish but not sticking to the mixing bowl.

Cut with a large cookie cutter & brush tops with milk. Place on a floured baking pan. Bake in a hot oven at 450 F | 180 C for 15 - 20 min.

Note   If using butter or lard instead of sour cream add a dash of lemon juice.

Serves about 24

Chocolate Fudge Cake

* 2 cups flour
* 3 tsp. baking powder
* ½ tsp. bicarbonate (optional)
* ½ cup butter
* 3 squares bitter chocolate, melted
* 1 cup sugar
* 2 egg yolks, well beaten
* 1 tsp. vanilla
* 1½ cup milk
* 2 egg whites, stiffly beaten

Sift all dry ingredients together.
Cream butter thoroughly, add sugar gradually &
cream until light & fluffy. Add egg yolks & melted
chocolate. Add flour alternating with milk, small
amounts at a time. Beat each time until smooth..
Add vanilla & fold in egg-whites.

Bake in 2 buttered & floured 23 cm | 9 in. cake pans
for 30 min.
Spread fudge frosting between the layers.

Apple Raisin Cake

In 1st bowl, mix well:

* 2 eggs
* 2 cups brown sugar
* ½ cup oil
* 1 tsp. vanilla

Add:

* 4 granny smith apples, cut in cubes
* 1 cup raisins or 1 cup chopped nuts

In 2nd bowl, sift:

* 2 tsp. baking powder
* ½ tsp. salt
* 1 tsp. cinnamon
* ½ tsp. cloves

Stir contents of 2nd bowl into the 1st one.
Place in well buttered pan & bake at medium temperature for ½ to ¾ of an hour.

For Icing, mix:

* ½ cup confectioners sugar
* 2 tbsp. Maple Syrup

Note   You can substitute 1 tsp. baking powder for:

* ¼ tsp. baking soda
* ½ tsp. cream of tartar

Orange Cake

Beat until creamy:
* 150 g butter

Add, beating well:
* 1 ½ cups + 2 tbsp. sugar

Always beating, add:
* 5 egg yolks

Sieve:
* 2⅓ cups modified flour
* 2 tsp. baking powder
* ¼ tsp. salt

Add alternating with the dry ingredients:
* juice & rind of ½ an orange

Incorporate:
* 5 egg whites, stiffly beaten

Pour into buttered baking pan & put in a 350 F | 175 C oven for 40 min.

For the Syrup mix & boil 5 min:
* 2 cups orange juice
* 1 cup sugar
* 1 cup water

Immediately you take cake out of oven (before taking it out of pan), pour syrup over it. Let it cool in the pan.

Note   To make modified flour sieve 3 times:
* 5 cups of regular flour with
* 1 cup cornflour

Brownies

* 113 g bitter chocolate
* 75 g butter
* 2 cups sugar
* 4 eggs (for chewy brownies use 1 egg less)
* 1 cup flour
* ¼ tsp. salt
* 2 tsp. vanilla

Melt in bain-marie:

* chocolate
  Remove from heat

Add:

* butter
  Stir until melted

Add:

sugar, eggs (unbeaten), salt & flour (chopped nuts optional) & vanilla.

Spread in a shallow pan, lined with heavy wax paper. Bake for 20 min at 350 F | 175 C. Remove from oven and cut in squares whilst still in the pan and hot.

Makes about 25

Concentrated Lemonade

Great on hot days, when it is too hot for tea.

* 4 lemons
* 1 kg sugar
* 2 tbsp. tartaric acid
* ½ litre boiling water

Peel the lemons, taking only a very thin layer off.
Then squeeze out the juice.
Place the thin lemon skin, juice, sugar & tartaric acid
in a large bowl & add boiling water. Leave overnight.
Stirring often.
Sieve the following day & pour into litre bottles.

This lemon essence keeps well without refridgera-
tion. Pour a measure into a glass & add cold water
to taste.

Makes about 2 litres

Emergency Menus

Dixieland Pie

* 1 tin sweet corn
* 6 hard boiled eggs
* 400 g diced ham
* ½ to 1 litre white sauce

In a buttered pyrex bowl place half the corn. Cover with 3 sliced hard boiled eggs. Cover with half the diced ham. Pour half the white sauce on it. Repeat the steps.

Top with fresh bread crumbs and dot with butter. The trick to this dish is to make a very tasty white sauce, such as adding grated cheese, a vegetable bouillon cube, salt, pepper & nutmeg to it.

Cook in a hot oven for about 20 min, until the top is nicely browned.

Serves 4 - 5

Cheese Soufflé

Rush a soufflé to the table the minute it's done,
especially if it's baked the french way - crusty
outside but soft and creamy within.

Melt:

* 4 tbsp. butter

Blend in:

* 4 tbsp. flour

Add gradually:

* 1 cup milk

Stir until thick and smooth.

Add:

* ½ tsp. salt
* few grains cayenne
* ½ to 1 cup grated cheese (Parmesan or a
  combination with camembert, swiss or
  bleu cheese.)

Stir until smooth and remove from the heat.

Add:

4 egg yolks, beaten until light
Cool, just before baking beat until stiff 4 eggs
whites (5 for a very fluffy soufflé) stir a tbsp. of the
egg whites into the yolk mixture. Fold in the rest.
Spoon into an unbuttered 1 ½ litre straight-sid-
ed baking dish. Set in a pan of hot water. For a
firm soufflé, bake 30- 45 min at 325 F | 170 C. For a
creamy soufflé (French version), bake 25 min at 375
F | 190 C. For a heartier soufflé, add diced ham and
sautéed mushrooms, or diced turkey or chicken.

Serves 4

Accompaniment for a
Quick & Tasty Pasta

* 1 large butternut squash
* head of garlic, chopped
* olive oil
* any good pasta, cooked al dente

Chop the butternut squash into cubes. Heat a large oven pan with 4 tbsp. olive oil. Place your butternut squash in it, & mix well. Sprinkle with salt & the head of chopped garlic.

Cook in hot oven for about 20 min, turning the cubes once or twice during the cooking, until they are slightly browned, they shrink as they cook & they stick, which adds to the flavour.

Serve piled on top of the pasta.

Serves 6

Matambre a la Leche (Brisket)

* whole milk
* 1 medium brisket
  with most of the fat removed

Place in an oven pan & cover with boiling water & put into a hot oven for half an hour. Then throw away the water & cover with full fat milk. Return to the oven.

When hot add:

* oregano
* 2 bay leaves
* 2 sprigs of rosemary

Return to the oven. In about ½ an hour, turn the brisket, if milk does not appear to be curdling add a dash of lemon juice. As necessary add more milk to keep it moist. The milk will start adhering to the pan, scrape it to prevent burning, and lower the temperature of the oven. A medium brisket will take about 3 hours to cook & be tender with occasionally turning it to toast on both sides. Before serving sprinkle with white pepper. Serve with the curdled milk as gravy. Best accompanied with fluffy mashed potatoes.

Serves 4 - 6

Mini Steaks

Place on a very lightly buttered hot skillet:
* mini steak 3 cm | 1 in. thick

When a bubble of blood shows on the top side, (this happens in about 3 - 4 min), flip the steak over & put a nob of butter on it.

Cook for a further 3 - 4 min.
Dust with salt & freshly ground black pepper & place on a hot serving dish. Dribble a little stock on the hot pan, and pour over steak as you serve.
You can wrap a rasher of bacon around the steak & secure with a toothpick. If you do this you have to go rolling the steak on a hot skillet to crisp the bacon before you start cooking it.
The meat should be rare in the centre & toasted on the outside.
Eat immediately!

Chicken Egg Drop Soup

* 1 tbsp. + 2 tsp. cornstarch
* 3 tbsp. white wine
* 1 tbsp. soy sauce
* 5 cups chicken stock
* ½ tsp. sugar
* 230 g cooked chicken breast, diced
* 6 green onions, shredded
* 2 eggs
* 1 tbsp. plus 1 tsp. all-purpose flour
* green onion curls to garnish

In a large saucepan, combine:

* cornstarch, wine & soy sauce

Pour in:

* stock

Slowly bring to a boil. Then simmer for 2 min.

Add:

* Chicken, shredded green onions & eggs

Simmer 2 - 3 min.

Serves 4 - 6

Banana Cream Syllabub

* 3 ripe firm bananas
* 2 tbsp. lemon juice
* 2 tbsp. white wine
* 2 tbsp. caster sugar
* 1⅓ cup thick cream

Peel the bananas, then mash with the lemon juice, wine & sugar.

Whip the cream until it holds its shape. Fold into the banana mixture.

Spoon into serving dishes & sprinkle with grated lemon rind. Chill before serving.

Serves 4 - 6

Jellied Fruit Snow

* 1⅓ cup thick sweetened fruit purée
* 1 tsp. powdered gelatine
* 2 tbsp. water or fresh fruit juice
* ⅔ cup thick cream
* 3 egg whites

Warm the purée gently, soften the gelatine in the water or fruit juice. Mix with the purée, stir until dissolved. Allow to cool, fold in half the lightly whipped cream & 2 stiffly beaten egg whites.

Spoon into 4 to 6 serving glasses & allow to set lightly (this will never be sufficiently stiff to turn out). Whip the remainder of the cream & the third egg white in separate bowls, fold together & pile on top of the dessert.
Decorate with grated lemon peel or slices if wished.

Serves 4 - 6

Cherub Peaches

* 50 g butter
* ½ cup soft brown sugar
* ¾ cup sweet white wine
* 1 cinnamon stick
* 4 peaches, skinned, halved & stoned
* 1 tbsp. cornflour
* 4 tbsp. water
* 1 tbsp. brandy

Place the butter, sugar, wine & cinnamon in a large saucepan & stir over a low heat until the sugar dissolves. Bring slowly to simmering point & add the peaches. Simmer for 5 min.
Blend the cornflour & water together until smooth, add to the sauce & bring to the boil, stirring constantly until the sauce thickens. Cook, stirring constantly, for a further 2 min then remove from the heat & stir in the brandy. Pour over the fruit.
Serve hot with single cream.

Serves 4

Fruit Ice Cream

Mash or blend:

* 1 cup of fruit
(Peaches, pears, strawberries or any other soft fruit).

Add:

* 2 egg whites, beaten until stiff

If using peaches or bananas, add:
* a dash of lemon juice

Add beating:

* ¼ to ½ cup sugar

Fold into fruit mixture and place in container in freezer.

For a grander ice cream you can add:

* 1 cup of thick beaten cream

Serves 4 - 6

Buffets

Tomato Jellies

* 750 g tomatoes
* 20 g gelatine
* 2 to 3 tbsp. water
* 1 tsp. salt
* ¼ tsp. celery salt
* ¼ tsp. pepper
* pinch sugar
* 2 tbsp. tomato purée
* 2 cups natural yogurt
* 1 tsp. sugar
* 3 to 4 tbsp. chopped parsley

Pour boiling water over the tomatoes, leave 2 - 3 min, then remove & peel. Chop the tomatoes & blend. Cover the gelatine with cold water & soak for 10 min, then heat to dissolve. Measure the tomato juice & dissolved gelatine & make up to 2½ cups with water. Pour into a saucepan, add half the salt, the celery salt, pepper & a little sugar. Whisk in the the tomato purée & heat gently. Rinse 4 - 6 small moulds with cold water & fill with the tomato mixture. Allow to set in the refigerator. Mix the yogurt, sugar remaining salt & the parsley together. Serve with the unmoulded jellies.

Serves 4 - 6

Spinach & Egg Cocottes

* 450 g fresh spinach
* 2½ cups water
* 3 tbsp. aspic jelly powder
* juice of ½ lemon
* 3 eggs, boiled until yolks are just set (5 min)
* 1 carrot, peeled & grated coarsely
* salt & pepper

Cut the stalks off the spinach & steam the leaves in a little salted water for 3 - 5 min until soft. Drain well & chop up finely. Bring the 2½ cups water to the boil, allow to simmer & dissolve the aspic jelly powder in it. Add the lemon juice to the dissolved aspic & leave to cool slightly.

Shell & coarsely chop the eggs & sprinkle with a little salt & pepper. Spoon a little aspic on to the bottom of the 8 cocotte dishes or deep patty tins.

Put in half of the chopped spinach & then the eggs & top with the remaining spinach. Spoon some of the aspic into these moulds, letting the contents absorb it & then add a little more. Strain the remaining aspic into a wide, shallow cake tin & stir in the grated carrot.

Leave to cool & then chill both the spinach moulds & the carrot aspic in the fridge. When chilled, dip the moulds briefly in hot water & shake out. Arrange on a serving dish. dip the cake tin of carrot aspic briefly in hot water, turn out & cut into little pieces. Use these to decorate all around the spinach moulds. Keep in the fridge until ready to eat.

Serves 4 - 6

Note A pinch of bicarbonate of soda when steaming vegetables enhances their colour.

Spinach & Garlic Terrines

* sunflower oil for greasing
* 450 g frozen chopped spinach, thawed
* 3 spring onions, sliced
* 2 cloves garlic, crushed
* 85 g grated cheddar cheese
* 3 eggs, beaten
* salt & freshly ground pepper
* watercress sprigs, to garnish

Tomato salad:

* 2 tsp. white wine vinegar
* 3 tbsp. olive oil
* 18 cherry tomatoes, halved

Preheat oven to 180 C|350 F. Lightly oil a loaf tin or a 4 ½ cup terrine. Line base & narrow ends of loaf tin with a strip of baking parchment.

Press as much water as possible out of spinach &
place in a blender or food processor. Add spring
onions, garlic, cheddar cheese, creme fraiche, eggs
& salt & pepper. Process until thoroughly blended.
pour mixture into prepared tin & cover with oiled
foil. Stand terrine in a roasting tin & add boiling
water to come halfway up sides of terrine. Cook in
the oven for 1 hour, or until a skewer inserted into
the centre comes out clean.

Leave to cool in the roasting tin. Pour out any of the
excess liquid from the terrine. Then chill for at least
2 hours.

Tomato salad:
Whisk together vineagar, oil & salt & pepper.
Toss tomatoes in dressing.
Turn out terrine & slice.
Garnish with watercress & tomato salad.

Serves 4 - 6

Savoury Banana & Watercress Salad

* 4 bananas
* juice of ½ lemon
* 1 bunch of watercress, chopped coarsely
* 2 tbsp. soured cream
* 1 tbsp. mayonnaise
* 2 tsp. top of the milk or single cream
* cayenne pepper
* grated nutmeg salt

Peel & slice the bananas & put in a bowl, adding the lemon juice & tossing around for a moment. Then add the chopped watercress.

In a small bowl mix the soured cream with the mayonnaise & single cream or top of the milk. Season well with salt, cayenne pepper & grated nutmeg to taste. Mix the dressing into the bananas & watercress & sprinkle with a little extra cayenne on top.

Serves 4

Red Bell Pepper Tart

Filling:

* 3 red bell peppers, cut in julienne strips
* 2 large tomatoes, peeled and chopped small
* 2 garlic cloves or more, finely chopped
* a good dash of vinegar + 4 tbsp. oil
* salt & pepper
* 1 tbsp. sugar

Put all ingredients in a bowl, and then leave to marinate for 2 - 4 hours.

Dough:

* melt 100 g butter in a pot.

Add to this & mix with a wooden spoon:

* 1¾ cup sifted flour
* 1 tsp. baking powder

In a cup mix:

* 1 tbsp. salt
* 2 yolks
* ¼ cup milk

Add to the dough mixing well. When it no longer adheres to the pot, it is ready. Spread on a pyrex tart dish. It spreads easily with fingers, as it's warm. Put the filling in & cook in a moderate oven for 45 min. Best served cold.

Carpaccio

* 1 kg fillet steak

Clean & remove fat.
Then freeze in a horizontal position,until hard, but
not frozen.

Cut in very thin slices & place them on large platter.

Sprinkle all over:
* 1 whole head of finely chopped garlic
* drizzle with olive oil &
* lemon juice (the juice of about 1 lemon)
* season with salt & pepper

Tightly cover with foil & place in refrigerator.
Best made the day before you serve. Decorate with
cherry tomatoes.
Good for hot summer nights.
Serve with cold salads.

Serves 6

Fruit Salad

In a large bowl, chop:
* 3 oranges (peel them, then cut into the centre of the orange & remove each segment without the inner skin)
* ¼ kg quartered strawberries
* 3 sliced bananas
* 2 tbsp. lemon juice
* 3 green apples diced
* 3 peeled peaches diced or
* ½ tin of peaches

Add sugar to taste. This brings out the flavour of the fruit.
Other fruits can be added in season, such as:
* pears, plums & kiwis.

Serve with fresh cream.
Calculate 2 fruits per person.

Serves 6

Banana Mint Meringue
Ice Cream Cake

* 200 g icing sugar
* 3 large eggs, separated
* 2 to 3 drops peppermint essence
* 225 g bananas
* juice of ½ lemon
* 175 g demerara sugar
* 6 tbsp. water
* 300 ml double cream
* shavings of plain chocolate, to decorate
* a pinch of salt

Sift icing sugar into a bowl. Whisk the egg whites in a large bowl until they stand in soft peaks and then whisk in the sifted icing sugar, a little at a time. Put the bowl over a large pan half-filled with gently simmering water and continue whisking for about 5 min until the meringue mixture is very stiff. Add in the peppermint essence. Heat the oven to 300 F | 150 C. Put a large sheet of greaseproof paper on to a baking sheet and spread the merigue mixture over it about 2 - 5 cm thick. Put the baking sheet on to the bottom shelf of the oven & cook until the meringue is firm & dry - at least 1½ hours. Allow to cool.

Ice cream:

Purée the bananas with the lemon juice until
smooth. Whisk the egg yolks, with the salt, until
pale and thickly creamy. Dissolve the sugar in the
water in a pouring saucepan over a low heat. Then
boil fiercely for 3 min and pour immediately in a
thin stream on the egg yolks, whisking all the time
at high speed. Continue whisking for at least 5
min until it is pale & thick, then beat in the banana
purée. In another large bowl whisk the cream until
thick but not stiff. Pour the banana & egg yolk mixture into the cream & fold in thoroughly with a large
metal spoon. Now turn the cooked meringue upside
down.

Peel off the greaseproof paper & then break up the
meringue, just roughly. In a deep 20 cm | 8 in. cake
tin make layers of the ice cream mixture & the broken meringue, starting & ending with a layer of ice
cream. Freeze.

When well frozen turn the ice cream cake out on to
a serving plate by rubbing the outside of the tin with
a hot cloth until it slips out.
Sprinkle shavings of plain chocolate on the top &
refreeze until ready to eat.

Serves 10

Tarte Montmartre

Pastry:

* 1¼ cup self-raising flour or
* 1½ cup plain flour + 2 ½ tsp. baking powder
* 1 tbsp. icing sugar

Melt:

* 100 g butter
* 1 tbsp. water

Mix with dry ingredients to form dough & spread on a 24 cm | 9.5 in. loose based tin & chill for ½ hour.

Filling:

* 3 eggs, separated

Whisk the egg yokes with:

* 3 tbsp. caster sugar

Gradually add:

* juice of 2 lemons
* 4 tbsp. cream
* 1 tbsp. cornflour

When smooth stir in:

* finely grated rind of 1 lemon

Apart whisk the egg whites until they form soft
peaks & fold gently into lemon butter.
Pour mixture into the pastry case & bake for 20 - 25
mins in a 350 F|180 C oven.

Chocolate Icing:

* 73 g|2½ bars dark chocolate + 1½ tbsp.
  water
* 4 tsp. caster sugar over very low heat

When smooth remove from heat & stir in:

* 2 tsp. cold water

Pour over tart & when cool decorate with:

* lemon rind, grated coarsely, or
* julienne strips of lemon rind

Serves 8

Ice Lemon Soufflé in a Chocolate Case

* 175 g plain chocolate + extra to decorate
* 3 tbsp. water
* 15 g butter
* grated rind + juice of 2 large lemons
* 4 large eggs, separated
* 15 g gelatine
* 1½ cup double cream

Oil a 19cm | 7.5 in. loose-based cake tin well & line the base with a disc of oiled greaseproof paper. Break up the chocolate & melt with 1 tbsp. of the water in bain-marie. When melted stir in the butter. Spoon the chocolate on to the base of the cake tin & spread evenly with a spatula all over the bottom & up the sides of the tin, leaving a rough & uneven edge. Leave to become firm while you make the soufflé.

Add the grated lemon rind & the caster sugar to the egg yolks & whisk until the mixture is pale & thick.

Squeeze the lemon juice into a saucepan & add the remaining 2 tbsp. of water. Sprinkle in the gelatine & dissolve in the liquid over a gentle heat but don't let it boil.

Pour the hot liquid slowly on to the egg yolk mixture, whisking all the time, until cooled a bit & just beginning to thicken. Whisk the cream until thick but not stiff & fold into the lemon mixture. Then whisk the egg whites until they stand in soft peaks & fold in with a metal spoon.

Pour into the chocolate-lined tin - the edge of the chocolate should be a little above the top of the soufflé. Freeze for at least 2 hours. To unmould, rub the sides of the frozen tin with a hot cloth & then, using a small & very sharp knife, cut down between the chocolate sides & the tin until it is loosened enough all round to push up. (The easiest way is to put the tin on top of a jam jar & then push down.)

Separate the chocolate base from the base of the tin with a knife if necessary & then carefully peel off the greaseproof paper. Put on a serving dish & refreeze until about 1 hour before you eat; then decorate the soufflé top with chocolate shavings and move the soufflé to the main part of the fridge, as it is to be eaten very cold, but not frozen.

Serves 8

Tidbits & Snacks

Homemade Pesto

* 50 g fresh basil leaves (or parsley)
* 4 to 5 cloves garlic, crushed
* 1 tbsp. pine kernels or nuts
* 6 tbsp. olive oil
* 25 g pecorino romano cheese or
  any good strong tasting cheese

In blender put basil, garlic, pine kernels & olive oil together with some salt. Blend to a smooth purée.

Then put into a bowl & stir in grated cheese.

Make in large quantities.
Freeze to have out of season.

Pâté de Paloma San Patricio

* 15 dove breasts
* 4 rashers of bacon
* ¼ cup of butter
* ½ sliced onion.
* 2 tbsp. lemon juice
* 2 tbsp. Lee & Perrins
* 2 tbsp. brandy
* salt & freshly ground black pepper
* dash of white pepper

On a hot skillet braise both sides of the dove breasts, remove from heat. In the same pan, fry the bacon until crisp. Remove & fry the onion in the bacon fat until golden. Remove & melt butter in the same pan.

Now blend the dove breasts, bacon & onion. Reduce to a paste. To this mixture thoroughly blend in the butter, lemon juice, lee & perrins & the brandy. Add salt & pepper & adjust seasonings to taste, more lemon juice or brandy can be added.

Serve with crisp toast or biscuits - can accompany cocktails, or as a start to a meal.

Serves 6

Baked Garlic

Delicious to serve as a dip with tiny bite size toasts.

Slice the top off:
* 12 to 15 heads of garlic.

Set together in a shallow baking dish & drizzle with a fine stream of fruity olive oil.

Sprinkle with salt & pepper & dried thyme.
Bake in moderate oven 350 F | 180 C for 25 min.
Then lower to 225 F | 110 C & bake for another 45 min **to an** hour until the garlic is mushy.

Dip out with a knife & spread on hot bread or toast.
Serve with red wine.

Serve 4 - 5 Toasties per head of garlic

Gruyère Puffs with Green Mayonnaise

Profiterols:

* 150 g plain flour
* 1 tsp. salt
* ¼ to ½ tsp. cayenne pepper
* 300 ml water
* 3 eggs
* 100 g gruyère cheese, grated
* mayonnaise
* 3 cups fresh or frozen peas
* a large handful of fresh mint leaves
* 4 tbsp. single cream
* ½ to 1 whole nutmeg, grated
* 1 to 1⅓ cup mayonnaise
* salt & black pepper
* 1 lettuce, to garnish
* 2 to 3 tomatoes, to garnish

Sift the flour, salt & cayenne pepper into a bowl. Put the water & butter in a heavy saucepan & bring to the boil, stirring until the butter has melted.

When boiling, tip in all the flour at once & beat with a wooden spoon until smooth. Continue beating vigorously until the mixture leaves the sides of the pan. Remove from the heat, beat in the eggs one at a time, beating thoroughly between each, and continue until the mixture is smooth and glossy. Beat in all but 25 g of the cheese.

Heat the oven to 425 F | 220 C. Grease a large baking tray & spoon on dessert spoons of the mixture, a little apart. Sprinkle the reserved cheese on the tops of the puffs. Bake in the centre of the oven for 25-30 min until well puffed & a rich golden brown. Remove carefully with a spatula & cool on a wire rack.

Meanwhile, to make the green mayonnaise, cook the peas, & then drain & rinse them with cold water to cool. Put them in a liquidiser with the mint leaves & single cream. Whizz to a thick mush- it doesn't have to be completely smooth. Season well with the nutmeg, salt & black pepper. Transfer to a bowl, & mix with the mayonnaise.

When the puffs are cold, slit them down one side & spoon the mayonnaise fairly evenly into all of them. Either serve on individual plates on lettuce leaves garnished with thinly sliced tomatoes, or on one large serving dish garnished equally prettily.

Serves 12 average size puffs

Little Ham & Cheese Rolls

Combine:

* 2 cups flour
* 4 tsp. baking powder
* 1 tsp. salt

With:

* ⅓ cup butter
* ⅔ cup milk

Roll out to ½ cm | ¼ in. thickness & spread with butter & french mustard.
Cover this with slices of ham & grated cheese.
Roll up & slice.
Bake in buttered pan in hot oven 20 min.

Makes about a dozen.

Stuffed Cheese Shortbreads

Biscuits:

* 1⅓ cup plain flour, plus extra for rolling
* 1 tsp. salt
* ½ cup & 1 tbsp. fine semolina
* 100 g strong cheddar cheese, grated finely
* 113 g butter, kept at room temperature

Spread:

* ¾ cup cream cheese
* 1 tbsp. chopped chives or spring onions
* black pepper

Heat the oven to 300 F | 150 C. Lightly grease a large baking sheet or tin. Mix the flour, salt & semolina together in a bowl. Add the cheese & butter. Work the mixture together thoroughly with you fingers until you have a smooth dough.
Roll out about 1 cm thick on a floured board & cut into small biscuits with a 5 cm | 2 in. cutter or the rim of a glass. Arrange on the baking sheet & bake in the centre of the oven for 1 hour. Allow to cool a little & then transfer the biscuits to a wire tray to cool completely.

Cream cheese mixture:

Simply soften the cream cheese with a fork & mix in the chopped chives or spring onions & black pepper to taste. Use the mixture either to sandwich together the biscuits or just to spread on top of them.

113

Serves 30

Dulce de Leche

The national south american jam, beloved of children. An accompaniment for rice pudding, cakes, bread & butter, or just spoonfuls of it!

Pour:

* 2 litres of unpasteurized milk

into a large pan.

Add:

* ½ kg sugar
* 1 tsp. bicarbonate of soda

Put on stove top, stir well until the sugar is dissolved. Then stop stirring.
Let the milk come to a boil, keeping an eye on it, until it rises 3 times.

When it settles into a rolling boil, lower the heat & cook until jam consistency, stirring occasionally. This will take about 2-3 hours, depending on your stove. If the milk sticks at all, do not scrape the bottom. Add 1 tsp. vanilla extract as you remove it from the stove.
The finished product should be smooth & a rich caramel color.

Makes 1 Kg.

Irish Coffee

* 4 measures of coffee with sugar to taste
* 1 measure whiskey
* ¼ measure cream

Heat coffee.
Apart heat whiskey.
Beat the cream, till slightly thickened.
When whiskey gives the first bubble, remove from heat & set alight.
Pour whisky into perfectly dry glasses.
Add coffee, then top carefully with cream, it should remain floating on top. If necessary pour cream over the back of a spoon
The idea is to drink the hot coffee through the cold cream.

Serves 4

Lele's Limoncello

* 7 large lemons
* 1 litre alcohol 95 proof (can substitute with vodka) lethaly strong stuff!
* 1¼ litres water
* 4 cups sugar

Peel lemons finely.
Soak peel in alcohol for a minimum of 4 days in a covered jar.
Make a syrup with the water & sugar. Boil for 5 min or more with the lid on until syrup forms.
Strain alcohol & mix with cooled syrup.
Bottle and place in freezer
Serve straight from the freezer.

Makes about 2 litres

Atholl Brose

Mix Well:

* 7 measures whisky
* 5 measures thick cream
* 1 measure honey

Serve in shot glasses as an after dinner liquor
(or traditionally with haggis!).

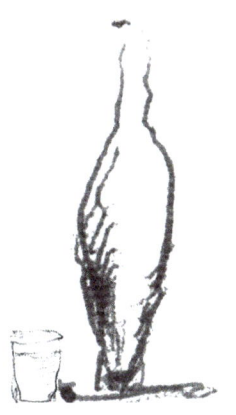

Special Occasions

Whisky & Honey Roast Chicken

* 1 chicken of 1½ to 2 kg
* 3 tbsp. honey
* 3 tbsp. whisky
* 60 g sliced & toasted almonds
* 2 tbsp. oil
* salt & pepper

Rub the chicken with whisky, season with salt & pepper (inside & out).
In baking dish place a sheet of aluminium foil to wrap chicken with.
Place the chicken on the foil and cover with honey (the breast & drum sticks). Sprinkle with the almonds. Baste with oil around the chicken. Wrap in the aluminium foil & place in a moderate oven 350 F|180 C for about 1¼ to 1½ hours.
Then open foil and allow to brown.
Good with a hearty bread stuffing.

Serves 4 - 6

Beef Tenderloin 'en croûte'

Clean & trim a whole tenderloin (about 1.2 kg).

Heat:
1 tbsp. oil, with:
* 2 crushed garlic cloves
* 1 teasp dried mixed herbs
* freshly ground black pepper

Brown the beef on all sides (about 5 min) then remove.

When cool, make the pastry with:
* 2 cups plain flour
* pinch of salt
* 100 g butter or fat
* ½ cup water

Roll out & spread with:
* pâté de paloma (page 108)

Or forcemeat made with:

* 1 tbsp. olive oil
* 1 clove garlic
* 1 large onion (or 2 shallots)
* fresh or dried tarragon
* 200 g pork sausage meat

Place the beef on top & wrap the pastry around it, sealing the ends. Put on lightly greased roasting pan & brush with egg to glaze. Bake in hot oven for 25 min then lower heat & leave a further 15 min for rare beef, or a further ½ hour for well done meat.
Serve immediately, cut in thick slices.
Good accompanied with onions lightly browned in butter & sautéed mushrooms.

Serves 4 - 6

Note   If your pastry is very flaky, roast in a bread pan as it will help hold its shape.

Gâteau Dianne

Meringue:

* 4 egg whites
* 1 cup + 2 tbsp. sugar
* 1 tbsp. instant coffee

Prepare 4 sheets of parchment paper of more or less 20x30 cm | 8x12 in, painted with oil. Place on cookie sheets.
Beat the egg whites until very firm.
Add 4 tbsp. sugar & keep beating until firm again.
Sieve the rest of the sugar along with the coffee & mix carefully into egg whites.
Spread evenly over the paper sheets & sprinkle with sugar.
Cook for 2 to 2½ hours in low oven 180 F | 90 C.
When ready carefully peel off the paper, let cool down.
Beat until creamy:

* 220 g butter

Have

* 4 egg yolks, well beaten

In a pan, dissolve slowly without allowing it to come to a boil:

* 1 cup + 4 tbsp. water
* 1 cup + 2 tbsp. sugar

Once the sugar has dissolved, bring it to a quick boil. When the a syrup forms a thread, slowly add to the well beaten egg yolks, beating constantly. Keep beating until it is cold, creamy & thick.

Slowly melt

* 1 tbsp. black coffee
* 100 g grated chocolate

Then as you keep beating, mix that into the creamed butter.

Spread the meringue layers with this cream, placing one above the other & add grated chocolate to the top layer.

This cake must be kept refrigerated for at least 24 hours before it's served.

Serves 8

Note Avoid making meringues on humid days (unless you want them to be chewy).

Milhojas

If you are not using commercially made pastry, make
your own with:
* heavy cream
* flour

Work together until the desired consistency and roll
very thinly on the base of a cake pan.
You need about 7 of these for a good sized cake.
Cook each one for about 5 min in a hot oven.
They should come out crispy and rather bubbly.
Put first layer on a cake plate, and spread with dulce
de leche.
Place another layer on top & repeat the operation
with the successive layers.
You can either make white mountain cream frosting
or royal frosting to ice the cake.
This cake can be kept in the freezer, the pastry
doesn't get soggy.

Royal frosting:

Put in a large bowl:
* 1 cup confectioners sugar
* ¼ tsp. cream of tartar
* ⅓ cup boiling water
* 1 egg white

Beat with an electric beater at high speed, until the frosting is thick enough to stand in peeks. This will take 8 min or more (it does no harm to interrupt the beating).

White mountain cream:

Put in a saucepan:

* 1 cup sugar
* ⅓ cup water
* ⅛ tsp. cream of tartar
* a few grains of salt

Cook until the syrup spins a 6 in|15 cm thread. Cook slowly. To keep syrup from crystallizing cover for the first 3 min. Beat until stiff 2 egg whites pour the syrup slowly over the egg whites beating constantly until thick.

Add:

½ tsp. vanilla

Walnut Cream Pie

(Very rich!)

Pastry:

* 160 g butter
* 1 cup caster sugar
* pinch of salt
* 1 egg
* 2½ cups plain flour
* 1 egg yolk, beaten for glaze

Filling:

* 1 tbsp. butter
* 2 cups granulated sugar
* 2 cups walnuts, roughly chopped
* 1 cup double cream

Cream:

The softened butter with the sugar, salt & egg.
Sift the flour over the top & knead all the ingredients together to make a pastry dough.
Cover & leave for 2 hours in the refrigerator.
Roll out ⅔ of the pastry to line the base & sides of a 23 cm | 9 in. flan tin, allowing the pastry to overlap the top all the way round. Pre-heat the oven to moderately hot
200 C | 440 F.
Melt the butter in a pan, add the sugar & cook, stirring continuously, until it caramelises to a light golden brown.
Add the walnuts & cream (be careful as it boils up) & bring to just below boiling point. Allow to cool then spread into the pastry case. Roll out the remaining pastry to make a lid, brush the overlapping sides with egg yolk & press on to the pastry lid to seal.
Brush the top of the pie with egg yolk & prick several times with a fork.
Bake for 30 - 40 min Then cool on a wire rack.

Serves 6

Viennese Orange Shortbreads

* grated rind 1 large orange
* 1 cup plain flour
* 1 cup cornflour
* ¾ cup butter
* nearly 1 cup sieved icing sugar

For filling & coating of icing sugar:

* grated rind of 1 large orange
* ¾ cup butter
* 1¾ cup sieved icing sugar

Put the grated orange rind into the mixing bowl.
Make certain you have taken just the top orange
'zest', not the bitter white pith that lies under the
skin.
Sieve the flour & cornflour into a small basin.

Add the butter & icing sugar to the orange rind & cream very well, by hand or mixer, until very soft & light. Gradually beat in the flour & cornflour.

Form 14 to 16 large neat round shapes on a buttered baking tray. Bake in the centre of a very moderate oven 170 C | 350 F, for about 15 - 20 min. They must crisp without becoming too brown. Allow to cool on the baking tray.

Cream the finely grated orange rind, butter & nearly all the icing sugar together.
Sandwich the biscuits together with the butter icing & dust with the remaining icing sugar.

Makes 7 - 8 Complete Shortbreads

Caramel Lemon Soufflé Almond Crunch

* 6 large eggs, separated
* 1 cup double cream
* juice of 2 lemons
* almost 1 cup water
* 15 g gelatine
* almost 1 cup granulated sugar
* 100 g flaked almonds
* 3 tbsp. caster sugar

Put the egg yolks in the bowl of a mixer & put the whites in another large bowl. Add the cream to the yolks & whisk.

Put the lemon juice & the 3 tbsp. water in a small saucepan, sprinkle in the gelatine & leave on one side.

Put the granulated sugar & the cup of water in a larger saucepan & dissolve the sugar over a low flame. Then increase the heat & boil fiercely for 4 - 5 min until pale brown, watching carefully so that it doesn't become too dark. Remove the pan from the flame.

Now put the saucepan containing the lemon juice &
gelatine over a gentle heat just to dissolve the gelatine.

Add this liquid to the caramel water & stir them
together until smooth. Bring to the boil again for a
moment & pour in a stream onto the cream & yolk
mixture, whisking all the time at high speed.
Leave in a cool place until cold & thick, stirring once
or twice.

Whisk the egg whites until they stand in soft peaks
& fold lightly into the cold caramel mixture with a
metal spoon. Pour in a wide 2.5 litre serving bowl
(glass looks pretty) & chill well in the fridge.

Meanwhile, put the flaked almonds in a bowl & stir
in the caster sugar. Heat an ungreased frying pan
until very hot, add the almonds & sugar & stir over
a high heat for just a minute or so until the almonds
caramelize to a rich golden brown. Turn them out
onto a large plate or a board & stir to separate them
as they cool & set, so that they don't stick together in
a mass. Just before serving scatter the almonds over
the top of the chilled soufflé.

Serves 8

Janis' Mousse de Menta

Beat until pale:
* 10 egg yolks

Make a syrup with:
* 1 cup sugar
* 1 cup water

Boil to fine thread stage.
Add the syrup to the yolks beating constantly.
Add a few drops mint essence (to taste).
Beat ½ litre heavy cream until thick. Fold into yolks.
Freeze. Serve unmolded with chocolate sauce.

Chocolate sauce:
Boil for 5 min:
* 30 g dark chocolate
* 2 tbsp. butter
* 1½ cup sugar
* Pinch of salt
* ⅓ cup water

Add:
* ⅓ cup heavy cream
* 1 tsp. vanilla

Serve immediately or keep warm in bain-marie.

Serves 4 - 5

Chemise

* 113 g butter
* ⅓ cup + 1 tbsp. caster sugar
* 150 g bitter chocolate melted
* sponge cake
* 2 eggs
* rum
* cream

Cream the butter & sugar & add the melted chocolate. Add the egg yolks.
Mix well.
Apart, beat the egg whites until stiff & fold in.
Line a 1/2 litre|2 cup mould with the sponge cake soaked in rum. Add the chocolate mixture & cover with more sponge.
Cover with a plate.
Put in the fridge.
Before serving turn out of the bowl & cover with whipped cream.

Serves 6

Brandy Snaps

* 100 g butter
* ⅓ cup + 1 tbsp. demerara sugar
* ¾ cup golden syrup
* a little less than ¾ cup plain flour
* 2 tsp. ground ginger

Put the butter, sugar & syrup into a saucepan & stir over a low heat until the sugar & butter have melted. Sift the flour & ginger together, add to the melted mixture & beat well until smooth.

Lightly grease a baking tray & , allowing for spreading, place 6 tsp. of mixtures on the tray. Keep the remaining mixture warm. Bake in the centre of a warm oven 160 C|325 F for 8 min or until pale gold. Leave for 1 min on the baking tray, then remove with a palette knife & roll the brandy snap round the handle of a wooden spoon so that the smooth side is outermost. Leave for 2 min to set, then slide off & cool on a wire rack. Repeat the procedure with the rest of the mixture.

Serve plain or filled with whipped cream.

Makes about 36

Index

Desserts

Cakes & Cookies

Drinks

Notes

CPSIA information can be obtained
at www.ICGtesting.com
Printed in the USA
BVHW020849090720
583332BV00015B/97